CW00376370

AVIATI⌐⌐ ⌐
PEOPLE MOVERS

by
Ken Davies

REGIONAL PUBLICATIONS, FRESHWATER, ISLE OF WIGHT

Printed by
THE WEST ISLAND GROUP
Afton Road, Freshwater, Isle of Wight, PO40 9TT

Published by
REGIONAL PUBLICATIONS
Afton Road, Freshwater, Isle of Wight, PO40 9TT

INTRODUCTION

Having sat down to write this introduction, it was a strange coincidence that when I glanced at my calendar I realised that in two days' time it would be exactly 97 years since Orville Wright made the first-ever flight by a manned and powered aircraft. His aircraft was more a 'person mover' than a 'people mover', but as it was the first, it seemed only reasonable to choose a picture to illustrate the events I have chosen on the following pages by starting at the beginning!

NINE DECADES AND 1500 MILES PER HOUR
OF AVIATION DEVELOPMENT

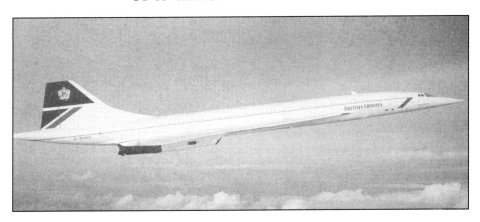

It is interesting to note that – apart from one-off speed record attempts, supersonic aircraft and space shuttles – it seems that average service speeds of passenger aircraft have only increased by something like sixty miles per hour for every decade of manned flight since Orville Wright started it all. It is said that his aircraft just about kept ahead of his brother Wilbur, who can be seen in the picture above running alongside!

It is also strange to consider that by far the largest flying machines of all time were most prolific in the first three decades of powered flight, and just how much bigger they were is shown clearly in the chart on the facing page.

The present generation looks to wide-bodied 'jumbo' jets as large, and the proposed Airbus A380 – with a capacity to carry over 500 passengers on two decks, non-stop for up to 8,000 miles in sixteen hours – is for us certainly very impressive. However, it is not the purpose of this book to be definitive, but rather to show some flexible logic in the various stages of the development of aircraft in just under a century to carry people or goods from A to B.

Maybe the following pages will stimulate a few to remember the pioneers and to recall a little more than which 'in-flight movie' they saw when going on holiday or travelling on business by air.

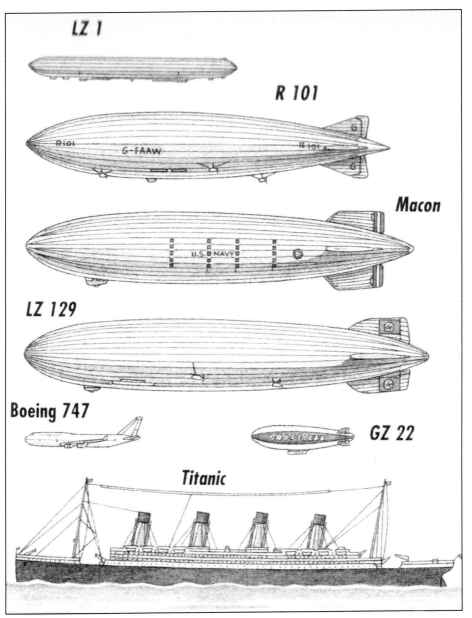

Early airships were the largest flying machines yet

THE FIRST THREE DECADES

In 1903, to coin a phrase, Orville Wright really started something – manned, powered flight. However, for all practical purposes it took two decades and a World War to make any serious 'people moving' by air possible. In Great Britain, Handley Page and Vickers adapted military bombers into crude and not particularly beautiful aircraft.

The idea of flight began to take a hold with the richer element of the population, in many cases just to show off. To cater for these there were attempts to match the service and comfort passengers had come to expect from other forms of travel. In the airliners of the late 1920s and '30s some of the standards aimed at were achieved.

It is noted that civil flying was developed from the technology forced on aviation by the years of the First World War, with the result that Germany made great strides in comfort and speed for long distance passengers by developing airships to great effect. It was only the use of highly inflammable hydrogen gas which brought about the disaster with the Hindenburg that put a sudden and very sad end to this attractive and marvellous form of air transport.

In Great Britain the lack of suitable airfields inhibited the operation of large and heavy aircraft being developed in the USA, where space and distance dictated designs to suit their particular internal needs. We in Britain concentrated on the short distance routes, mainly from London across the Channel to Paris, and flying boats were the only practical solution for our 'Empire Routes'.

In common with America we had the Atlantic on one of our borders, which was an incentive to develop long-distance flying boat type aircraft with comfort for passengers and speed for mail. America had the Pacific on its western coast which was an added incentive, with the result that both countries produced some very elegant and practical flying boats in the late 1930s. The unfortunate outbreak of the Second World War put an effective end to the development of civil flying for a further six years.

Two or three years after the end of World War I, and less than two decades after Orville Wright's historic flight, tentative efforts were made to produce aircraft to carry passengers and not bombs. Inevitably manufacturers had to lean on such experience gained during the war, as transporting passengers by air wasn't considered possible prior to the outbreak of hostilities. Handley Page introduced the W8c in 1921 and produced some twenty or more with capacity for up to sixteen passengers in a reasonably large cabin.

Vickers produced forty-four 'Vimy Commercials' in 1921 which could carry up to ten passengers. Both aircraft had two Rolls Royce 'Eagle' engines and a range in the order of 500 miles at a speed of just over 100 miles per hour.

THE ARMSTRONG WHITWORTH ARGOSY OF IMPERIAL AIRWAYS

Four of the Armstrong Whitworth Argosy airliners were built specially for Imperial Airways and entered service between Croydon and Paris in 1926 – very practical aircraft, considering that aviation was only twenty-three years old at the time. These aircraft look strange to modern eyes, but they did cut the journey time between the capitals from six hours by train and ferry to about two and a quarter. Such was progress in the twentieth century!

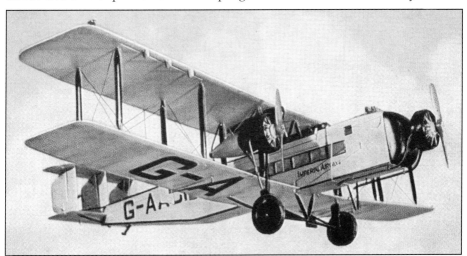

IMPERIAL AIRWAYS ARGOSY AT CROYDON c.1930

By 1925 the UK made the grade in an aircraft of reasonable carrying capacity with the three-engined Armstrong Whitworth Argosy and, like Germany with its Junkers 38, certainly missed out on the beauty side. Anyway, 'beauty is in the eye of the beholder' and Imperial Airways managed to get twenty-six passengers into the air in something like comfort in each of their four Argosy airliners – a little noisy perhaps, but at least it wasn't sitting beneath a crude cover over an open cockpit.

THE JUNKERS G38

Considering the Junkers G38 made its maiden flight in 1929, just over a decade after the First World War, it certainly rates as a large 'people mover' of its time. No beauty, it could carry thirty-four passengers and rates as unique in their accommodation – twenty-six in the main fuselage, three in the leading edge of each wing root and two in the nose! Only two were built – one was lost in an accident and the other at the hands of the RAF in 1940 – but they were highly successful aircraft.

THE GERMAN GIANT OF THE 1930s

The giant German passenger airliner, the Junkers G38, proved to be the subject of intense interest when it visited Croydon in 1931. The picture above shows the situation of the unique passenger accommodation. Its sheer size, massive wings and four engines were a source of comfort for potential passengers who still considered that size and four funnels were a safety factor in ships, in spite of the *Titanic*!

THE MIGHTY DO-X

After World War I German industries were restricted in what they could produce, especially anything that could possibly be used as a weapon, so they had the DO-X flying boat built on the Swiss Lake Constance shore in 1925. She weighed nearly fifty tons and had a wing span of 157 feet, with twelve engines mounted in six tandem pairs.

THE DORNIER DO-X ON ITS WAY

When built she was easily the largest aircraft in the world and showed her capabilities with a demonstration which took her around the globe, including at least one call at Calshot. In point of fact two more were built for an Italian airline, but they were so under-powered and uneconomical to operate that they eventually went into military service in the early 1930s.

Whatever the critics said about them, they were the biggest and they did fly! Not for the first time, economics beat them. It is a story we have heard many times since.

DO-X INTERIOR

Considering the complexity of a twelve-engined aircraft, the flight deck looks amazingly simple when compared with a present-day aircraft of only two engines. However, the comfort and leg room for passengers might make modern airlines think a little further.

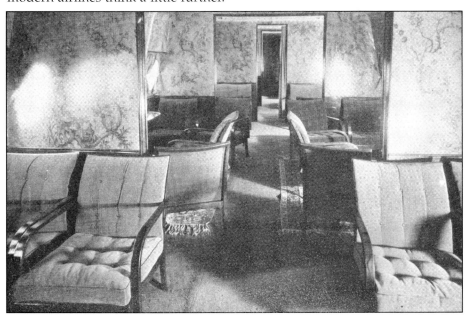

AIRSHIP TRAVEL IN THE EARLY 1930s

There is little doubt that travel by airship in the early 1930s as advertised by the German agencies left little or nothing to be desired, even by comparison with many of the shipping companies over the same routes. It was quicker, smoother and equally good as far as the creature comforts that were provided. The only thing that can now be said is what a pity helium gas was not available or used in those days.

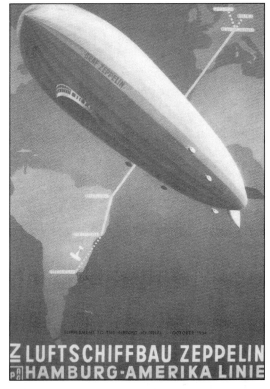

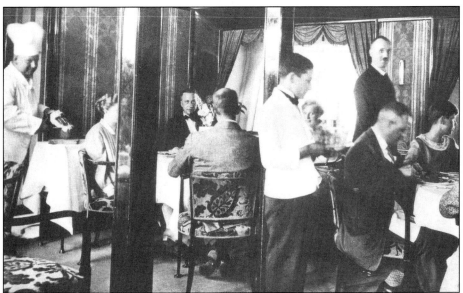

THE GRAF ZEPPELIN AND THE HINDENBURG

There is no doubt that Germany had the expertise and experience to produce and fly these giant aircraft. It gave a totally new aspect and opened possibilities that offered trans-oceanic travel at a speed never known before, by advertising a two-day voyage to North America. The Graf Zeppelin, above, and Hindenburg, below, were the peak of development of what was hoped would be opposition to ocean liner travel, and the first few flights were a sensation with praise lavished on them by all who experienced them and those who hoped to. The crash of the R101 and the Hindenburg catastrophe in 1937 put a complete end to travel by airship, and it hasn't recovered to this day.

PASSENGER-CARRYING AIRSHIPS (1920s–1930s)

Early airships were little better than powered and steerable balloons built and developed for military purposes. However, in the 1920s the British and the Germans built what were the largest passenger-carrying aircraft, a fact which still exists to this day. The two largest British machines were the R100, seen above during an amazingly successful flight to Canada. The R101, in the picture below, was her slightly larger sister. The praise lavished on her at first was soon to be forgotten when she met with a disaster in the early stages of a demonstration flight to India in 1930. She flew into a hill near Beauvais, killing all but eight of the fifty-plus passengers and crew on board under what to this day seems to be suspect circumstances as to why the flight was allowed to go ahead.

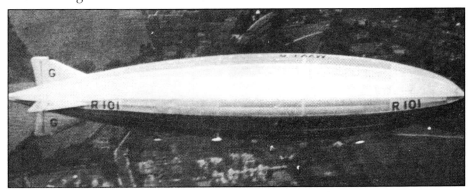

IMPERIAL AIRWAYS' LAST LARGE BIPLANE AIRLINERS, THE HP42s

The Handley Page HP42s were the last of the biplane passenger aircraft built for Imperial Airways in the 1930s, the purpose being to replace the smaller and ageing Argosies. Some said they were elegant, others said they had a built-in headwind. Regardless of these comments, the HP42s gave passenger comfort over three continents and some survived to give service in the first year or so of the Second World War. They will long be held as examples which demonstrated to the public that air transport was here to stay.

SLOW SPEED AND COMFORT IN THE 1930s

The Handley Page airliners of the 1930 vintage were popular mainly because of their reliability and comfort. The picture below is not very good, but it is the best we have. However, it does give an insight into the type of 'Pullman' comfort that was expected by those who could afford to fly in the late 1930s.This was maintained, apart from the War years, by Imperial Airways and later BOAC until the 'Jet to the Med' took over with a demand for cash in place of leg room. The result has been that only those on expense accounts or who can afford the cost of first-class travel can still have space to stretch their legs in these days, with some flights of up to eighteen hours in the air.

SHORT'S NON-IDENTICAL TWINS
OF THE EARLY THIRTIES

In the early 'thirties Short Brothers produced the Short Scylla, seen above, for Imperial Airways which was in effect a near-twin to the Short Kent shown below. At the time they had some radical features. Their passengers were accommodated in luxury and meals were served on board. Even the crews were treated well, they had covered cockpits, and, oh yes, one was a flying boat! The flying boats were replaced by the Empire 'C' class a few years later, but the Scyllas saw service as transports for a short while after the outbreak of World War II.

PEOPLE MOVERS OF THE EARLY THIRTIES

A Lufthansa Junkers JU52

The Junkers G38 preceded the tri-motor JU52 by four or five years, but its smaller and younger sister probably moved tens of thousands of people in both its civil and military form. Its reputation for reliability and safety made it popular in both forms, but became notorious during the Second World War when used as a troop carrier and communications aircraft, when Germany invaded many of the very countries it had served in earlier, more peaceful times. A few are still flying to this day, six decades later!

Below is part of a gathering of nearly thirty aircraft at Croydon in 1933. The KLM Fokker nearest the camera has a couple of Air France Wibault 282s ranged alongside, giving a perfect gathering of aircraft of that era's vintage.

A Fokker FXX and two Wibault 282s at Croydon in 1933

22

Westland Wessex

The Wessex and Cruiser were both examples of aircraft considered to be suitable for building up intensive local and short haul stages where loadings were light and frequency of service important in the early 1930s. Unfortunately, in the British Isles it was the unreliability of our climate, not the aircraft, that added to the after-effects of the great depression of the 'twenties and 'thirties which gave such a short life to attempts to set up good internal services. However, the two aircraft on this page found a limited favour abroad and to include them is to illustrate a trend in air travel in the early 1930s.

Spartan Cruiser Mk III

FOUR DECADES THAT CHANGED AVIATION

In Europe and especially Great Britain civil aviation was beginning to take a grip on the public's imagination. Light aircraft, club and private flying was becoming more popular, but passenger traffic was confined to relatively short journeys between the UK and the Continent. This type of traffic was operated mainly by old-fashioned biplanes which at the end of the 1930s were gradually being replaced by four-engined monoplanes like the AW Ensign class.

The demands for passenger traffic over the longer routes was limited but the pressing need was to speed up mail. Flying boats were introduced on these routes because even if we did have airfields that could have handled larger and heavier aircraft, the stopping points across the so called 'Empire Routes' certainly couldn't. To overcome the problem those marvellous four-engined Short 'C' class Empire flying boats were introduced. In spite of the interference of what was virtually a whole decade of war years, these flying boats and their derived versions lasted well into the 1950s until replaced by long-range, reliable, land-based aircraft that could master the longer stages including the lucrative transatlantic routes.

The 1950s showed the effect of the Second World War on civil aviation very clearly. The internal demands of the American market together with vast areas of land they could use to accommodate large heavy aircraft meant that they could lead the way with that type of aircraft, which they inevitably did! Great Britain had to build airfields for fighters and bombers in World War II which led to the situation where we had so many that cynics who flew over us later said, "From the air we looked like an aircraft carrier moored off Europe".

These left us with an over-abundance of airfields, many being just left to rot, but at least we could set up some really good airports at what were strategic places to cater for our own regional and internal civilian needs. At the same time we also re-entered the civil aircraft industry with some considerable gusto. The pity of it was that because of the vast internal market in the USA for larger aircraft they had us well beaten in the commercial sense for a couple of decades. We had some very good large aircraft which flew alongside the American planes, but in the end their domination of aviation's larger 'people movers' held sway the world over until Europe's main industrial countries joined forces in the joint production of large airliners in the 1980s and '90s which are just beginning to erode American dominance.

ARMSTRONG WHITWORTH AW27 ENSIGN

The Armstrong Whitworth AW27 Ensign class of airliner was the largest type built for Imperial Airways prior to the outbreak of the Second World War in 1939. Thirteen of these potentially great aircraft were ordered and entered service on a number of routes before being requisitioned for transport duties when hostilities started. Even today many pilots will say that if a plane looks good she will fly well. While this is not always right, the Ensigns did look good, even in service camouflage. Some time about 1941 they were re-engined and continued to give good service, some as far afield as Australia, until the end of the war. Then, survivors of the class were returned to the UK, sadly having long gone past their 'sell by' date for normal peace-time passenger work.

Two further views of the Armstrong Whitworth Ensign which clearly show its good-looking clean lines, even on the ground and in service colours. They also show the easy access which must have been a boon on remote airfields where ground service facilities were minimal. There is little doubt that had it not been for the Second World War they would have been a truly great passenger aircraft.

TRENDS IN THE LATE 1930s

Lockheed Electra

Although stretching the large 'people mover' theme on which this book is based, the Electra, some versions of which carried up to fifteen passengers, was a trend-setter on many domestic services the world over and indeed a 'people mover'.

De Havilland DH95 Flamingo

A British trend-setter of 1938, the Flamingo had a number of features that formed the basis for similar types that were to follow. They were De Havilland's first aircraft with an all-metal stressed skin, they had a retractable undercarriage and a passenger capacity of up to seventeen. The RAF ordered forty but these were cancelled on the outbreak of war and the majority of the sixteen produced remained in civilian hands.

TRENDS IN THE LATE 1930s

The Focke-Wulf Fw 200 Kondor

In 1938 Lufthansa's Kondor *Brandenburg* made a non-stop flight from Berlin to New York in twenty-four and a half hours, which satisfied Lufthansa's requirement for a long-range airliner with a capacity for twenty-six passengers. Had it not been for the outbreak of war in 1939 Kondors would probably have been among the first regular transatlantic aircraft in service. In the event they were taken over by the Luftwaffe as long-range oceanic reconnaissance aircraft – to the great cost of allied shipping.

Douglas DC2

The forerunner of the world famous DC3 (Dakota), the DC2 was a short/medium range aircraft and the first of over 12,000 'people mover' derivations, many still flying sixty years later.

THE FLYING BOAT ERA

The flying boat era as far as 'people moving' is concerned was concentrated in the two and a half decades from the early 1930s to the middle of the 1950s, but like many things the limits are hard to define.

Apart from situations where long distances over water were demanded, such as to Latin American countries from the USA, the main practical use for flying boats, apart from military needs, was in the speedy delivery of mail for the whole of the 1930s.

In America the mail services were handled by contracts, with a number of civil companies operating land planes. However the British requirements were different, as mail to outposts of the Empire was an essential part of our civil and military communications and people took second place until the mid 1930s.

Above:
Sikorsky S40 (USA)

Left:
Short Calcutta (GB)

The Short Calcutta is a typical early-1930 flying boat of Imperial Airways used on the Mediterranean stages of the early Empire mail flights to the East. These aircraft did on occasion carry passengers, but on the other hand the USA had many islands, and for the Latin American countries to the south travelling by sea was the only alternative to the flying boat.

The interesting point in aviation development is that there are still islands too small for even a crude airstrip and where a flying boat, albeit much smaller than many of the early ones, is still the only alternative to travel on the water rather than over it.

As the smaller flying boats of today are many and varied, it has been decided to concentrate on the larger aircraft used in this era so as not to confuse the 'people mover' theme adopted in this book.

SIKORSKY S42

The Sikorsky S42 was built as a long-range trans-oceanic flying boat with a capacity for from eight to thirty-two passengers according to the length of the flight. Entirely successful survey flights were made across the Pacific and Atlantic in 1934 and 1936 over a number of routes that provided the experience for the following scheduled services being promoted by Pan American and Imperial Airways in the two or three years before the outbreak of the Second World War in 1939.

The cutaway drawing shows clearly the four passenger compartments on a Sikorsky as Pan American would have operated her on some of the shorter stages. The four passenger compartments, each seating eight, would be much envied today. Up front there was a very adequate galley, spacious flight deck and quarters for the crew.

SIKORSKY S44

In 1940 an American airline started operating with Sikorsky VS44A flying boats between New York and Lisbon. With hindsight this was probably because at that time Portugal was a neutral country and America had not entered the war. This enabled a transatlantic route to be operated that didn't conflict with a war zone, which in the event carried on until 1945 when the flying boats were eclipsed by new land planes. It was an indication of the traffic that airlines were beginning to attract that from 1941 to 1945 over four hundred Atlantic crossings were made by these Sikorsky aircraft alone.

THE MARTIN M130 CLIPPER

Although only produced in very small numbers in the two or three years before the outbreak of the Second World War, the Martin Clipper was a very popular and successful aircraft. It had a maximum load of forty-six passengers (less on longer routes where sleeper accommodation was required) and would normally be operated by a crew of five. The war stopped further development when military demands had to take over the Martin company's production capacity.

PAN AM's TRANSPACIFIC ROUTES
1935 TO 1940

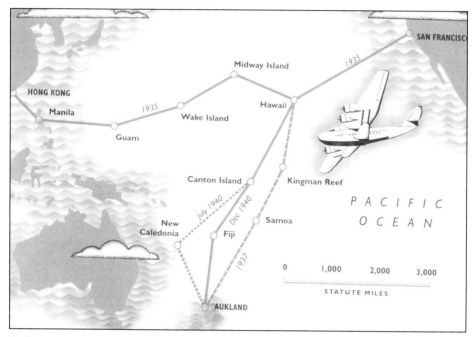

Below is a Pan Am China Clipper approaching for a landing at Manila on its inaugural flight in 1935, for which passengers paid over $1,400 for the round trip, then the equivalent of £450! The onward flight to Hong Kong meant a change of aircraft, probably a Sikorsky, which would have cost nearly as much again, an extra $1,300.

BOAC AND PAN AM TRANSATLANTIC ROUTES

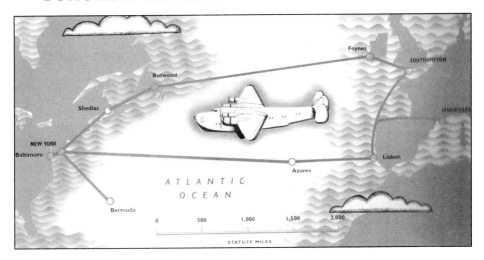

Early transatlantic routes were originally aimed at getting a rapid mail service, but war interfered with this and BOAC had three of the Boeing 314 Clipper flying boats. Together with some of the British Empire class aircraft, two routes were established over the North Atlantic. One of these was via Shannon and Botwood, shown in the picture below, which flew the more southerly route via Lisbon and the Azores after the outbreak of the Second World War in 1939, when the British terminal for civil operations was transferred from Southampton to the less busy waters of Poole Harbour.

BOEING 314 CLIPPERS

By 1939 Pan Am had six of these beautiful flying boats in service, three of which were on the non-stop flight from New York to Lisbon, the others on various Pacific routes. By June 1939 others were introduced, including two or three which were operated by BOAC. The one in the picture below was in fact used by Winston Churchill, the British Prime Minister, for a return from a meeting with President Roosevelt in the States in 1942. It is quoted that he took the controls for some time and said he got more and more attached to the flying boat.

BOEING CLIPPER'S INTERIOR

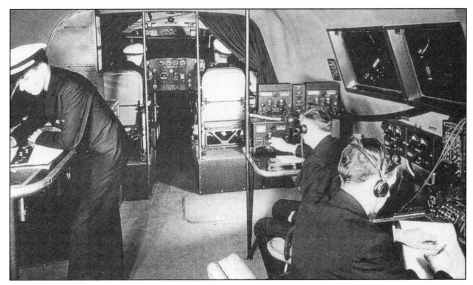

It is little wonder that Winston Churchill was impressed with the 314 flying boat because the flight deck was impressive enough, but like the British and other trans-oceanic aircraft of the 1930s and '40s their speed was normally just short of 200 m.p.h. A three thousand mile flight therefore took fifteen or more hours and the accommodation had to be good enough to encourage passengers to fly as an alternative to the luxury liners of the day, even to the extent that the Boeings had a dining room.

BOEING 314 CLIPPER IN BOAC LIVERY
AND A VIP ON BOARD

The long range of the Boeing 314s made them ideal for long-range flights, and the above picture shows the aircraft which brought Winston Churchill back from America with him at the controls, as seen in the picture below. One wonders how big a VIP one had to be in those days before you could be at the controls with a cigar in your mouth. Perhaps it wasn't alight!

THE SHORT COMPOSITE AIRCRAFT
MAIA AND MERCURY

The Maia and Mercury were built as a pair to experiment with small fast aircraft that could be launched with a load of fuel which would enable express mail service across the Atlantic. A number of successful test flights were made but the experiments had to be terminated late in 1938 because the transatlantic terminal at Botwood would ice up. War clouds loomed in 1939 and the idea was dropped. Maia was destroyed in an air raid in May 1941 and Mercury was broken up a few months later.

THE 'C' CLASS EMPIRE FLYING BOATS

By the mid-1930s the Postmaster General had introduced the Empire postal scheme whereby air mail letters could be sent to any country within the Empire for a flat rate of $1^1/_2$ old pence per ounce. On occasion a few passengers were flown on the routes where this was possible. At the same time Great Britain and the USA were trying to find a suitable aircraft for transoceanic passenger traffic, especially across the Atlantic. For our part Imperial Airways ordered 28 four-engined flying boats from Short Brothers for use on Atlantic and other Empire routes. These were the crowning glory for British Aviation of the era and became known as the 'Empire Boats'.

EMPIRE FLYING BOATS – OUR PRIDE AND JOY

The most luxurious Flying-Boat in the world

IMPERIAL AIRWAYS

From the late 1930s onwards the Empire Boats served in many capacities (including the war years) up to 1947. Until the outbreak of the war they were the height of fast luxury travel and gave considerable competition on many routes to the ocean liners of the day for those who could afford speed and comfort. Imperial Airways had 'the most luxurious flying boat in the world', a reputation they kept up when BOAC was formed, albeit with aircraft developed from the Sunderland which was a military development of the 'C' class aircraft. Most of the services from the British Isles were operated from Southampton Water, Poole and Shannon.

The 'C' class in the picture below was about to be sold to Australia in 1939 although in the end BOAC retained it for their operations.

THE SHORT S26 'G' CLASS

The first of this class, the *Golden Hind*, was introduced in 1939 for Imperial Airways' non-stop transatlantic services, but the outbreak of the Second World War prevented this. The *Golden Hind* and the two following boats, *Golden Fleece* and *Golden Horn*, were commandeered for long-range reconnaissance duties with Coastal Command. Although outwardly they looked to be similar to the Empire 'C' class aircraft, they were in fact considerably larger with improved performance, serving their military assignments very well until being returned to the newly-formed BOAC in 1941. After the loss of the *Golden Fleece* when two engines failed causing a forced landing, BOAC used them mainly on West African and Poole to Cairo services until old age caught up with them in about 1947.

THE SHORT SHETLAND FLYING BOAT

Designed as a long-range military flying boat, the prototype was destroyed at Felixstowe in 1946 and by that time the specification requirements had been changed and the second prototype was produced as a civil version. By the early 1950s BOAC were concentrating on the use of land planes and after a brief use as a flying test bed the massive Shetland was big and unwanted and scrapped in 1951, never having served any of the purposes for which it was designed.

THE SUNDERLAND, HYTHE AND SANDRINGHAM

The Short Sunderland flying boat was a direct military descendant of the Imperial Airways' Empire flying boats and first flew late in 1937. During the Second World War, Imperial Airways became BOAC and operated some Sunderlands to support the various transport needs over long water stages. Some of these were unarmed and carried civil registrations and continued to do so at the end of hostilities. Many were converted to civil use for BOAC and other airlines where their routes had no land-based airfields in areas like the South Pacific.

The civilianised Sunderlands became known as 'Hythes' and 'Sandringhams', depending largely on the details of the build or conversion. The upper picture on this page shows a Sunderland in wartime colour and a civil registration, and the picture below is one of the last Sandringhams flying, beached at Calshot just before restoration and preservation at Southampton.

THE SWAN SONG OF FLYING BOATS IN THE 1950s

The Sandringham above is the actual aircraft now preserved in the Aviation Museum at Southampton in the colours it flew with when operated by the Australian service to the offshore islands. It later went to the Caribbean to fly for Antilles flying boats before being flown to the UK as a private venture. About this time BOAC were still promoting flying boats but with a sneaky portent of things to come, hence the small indication of the Lockheed Constellation on the poster, right.

SHORT SOLENT

As the Second World War drew to a close, the hostilities became concentrated in the Pacific and Short Brothers upgraded the Sunderland for service in that area. A slightly larger version with more power, greater armament and more range was built with the name 'Seaford'. Out of the few that were built and saw service, one was loaned to BOAC for evaluation after hostilities ended and this resulted in them ordering twelve for civil use under the name 'Solent'. These saw service with a number of airlines until long-range land-based aircraft put most of the flying boats out of business in the late 1950s.

SHORT SANDRINGHAM

A number of Sandringhams, civilian versions of the military Sunderlands, served all over the world from the Southern Pacific to the West Indies. It was from Antilles Air Boats in the West Indies that two Sandringhams were later brought back to the UK. Of these, one is now preserved in pristine but non-flying condition and is open to the public at Southampton's Aviation Museum. The other is still in flying condition and has made a number of 'show off' flights around the UK, including Windermere in the Lake District, seen in the picture above, where thirty or more Sunderlands were built in the Second World War. This aircraft is now owned by a wealthy American who aims to keep it flying as long as possible.

The flight deck of the one preserved in Southampton, typical of these machines, is shown below.

THE H4 HERCULES – THE BIGGEST AIRCRAFT
EVER FLOWN

The H-4 Hercules remains to this day the largest aircraft ever to have flown. It had a 320 ft wing span, was designed to carry over 700 troops and had eight 3,000 h.p. engines. Built almost entirely of wood, it earned itself the name 'Spruce Goose'. Delays in construction and the fact that it was going to be under-powered meant that further progress on the three ordered was halted. However, Howard Hughes – determined to prove his point – did fly it in 1947 on its one and only flight at Long Beach, California, for a distance of just over a mile at a height of between seventy and a hundred feet. It was then kept in its hangar until 1981, since when it has been preserved and is on public display.

SPRUCE GOOSE

In this day and age when large 'jumbo' aircraft are common it is still hard to imagine the immense size of the 'Spruce Goose'. Perhaps the ground view of the aircraft on the shore is a good indication, but the picture of a small section of its interior tells its own story. On its very short and only flight it was piloted by Howard Hughes himself, without the help of the co-pilot and over thirty technicians and engineers who were on board.

THE BEAUTIFUL PRINCESS

The beautiful Princess flying boat was one of triplets, but sadly in medical language two were still-born. The fact was that 'progress' killed all three because commercialism took over before the Princesses had time to grow up. The one that did last long enough to take to her element logged over ninety hours of flying and made a great impression wherever she was seen.

The aftermath of the Second World War left many suitable airfields dotted around the world to take the more flexible land planes which were developed from wartime bombers and technology. This put the necessity for large flying boats right out of court. Even so, the Princess was a beautiful flying machine and was a landmark in British aviation in which we can all be justly proud.

PRINCESS FLYING BOAT

The Saunders Roe Princess was a rare bird of great size and great beauty in the air and on water. The crews who flew her found her faultless and enjoyed the space and layout of the flight deck as seen below. The public adored and were proud of what was to them a great British achievement. Not likely to be a commercial success through no fault of her own, the Princess will remain a part of British aviation history that will be remembered for many decades to come.

A HUNDRED HOURS IN THE LIFE
OF A BEAUTIFUL BIRD

It is easy to get emotional when the sight of an aircraft like the Princess was being shown off. Worse than that, from the public's point of view, was to watch the slow and undignified end where the three aircraft which were actually built, backed by so many great hopes for British aviation, were cocooned where all could see them, then eventually towed away for scrap.

PASSENGERS COULD 'LAND ON LAND'
ONCE HOSTILITIES WERE OVER

Even during World War II, as hostilities were drawing to a close, thought was being given to the regeneration of civil aviation in Great Britain by the 'Brabazon Committee'. This anticipated a growth in air transport at the end of hostilities, with aircraft being built to serve the public now that suitable airfields were available nationwide.

In some ways the Princess and the Brabazon aircraft were disasters. The Brabazon in particular was designed by inexperienced technicians and without the availability of modern computers and production techniques. The fact that it flew at all was a credit to the Bristol company and should never be forgotten as 'a good try under the circumstances'. At least other aircraft built to meet Brabazon specifications were good aircraft.

To be fair, the Princess was delayed by non-availability of engines when needed, and then overtaken by development of land-based aircraft which rendered it out of date.

Douglas DC3 (Dakota)

The recovery from war years was not as easy as it might have been, partly because of the demands of the Berlin Airlift. However, in Britain we made good use of that old aviation war horse, the Douglas DC3, known all over the world as the Dakota, or just 'the Dak'. Over 10,000 were built, so there were plenty about. There can be few airfields around the world which have not had a Dak call at some time. Even today there are more than just a handful still flying, six decades after the first one took to the air.

Taking another example, the Viking was a direct descendant of the Wellington bomber, using many parts such as wings, engines and tail units – and even the geodetic fuselage construction method. For a number of years after the war these gave good service to BEA and were even used for Royal flights. These types of aircraft kept our civil aviation going until new, larger and more reliable aircraft became available.

OFFERINGS FROM AVRO WHEN THE WAR WAS OVER

At the end of the Second World War, Britain was desperate to establish itself as a force to be reckoned with in civil aviation and set about using the basic parts of some of its successful bomber aircraft. The Avro York, pictured above, used many of the parts from a Lancaster bomber with a square, capacious fuselage added which gave it a strange squared-off look, with the high-wing configurations of the pre-war Armstrong Whitworth Ensign. Perhaps not the most attractive aircraft for passengers, it gave remarkable service in the Berlin Airlift of 1948.

The Avro Tudor 4 in the picture below was meant to be a more modern, pressurised airliner and was also developed using many parts from the war-time Avro Lancastrian bomber. At that time BOAC demanded so many changes in its development that it was never satisfactory and was highly suspect in operability, forcing early withdrawal from passenger service. It also served in the Berlin Airlift, as a cargo carrier.

THE LARGE AND BEAUTIFUL BRISTOL BRABAZON

The mighty Bristol Brabazon was first mooted in 1944 when the Brabazon Committee called for a design to fill a post-war need for a long-distance transatlantic four-engined airliner. Some thought it should never have been built as delays in construction and the lack of suitable available engines made the whole concept redundant. However, after many postponements, it did fly in 1949 – but other designs, turbine engines and a little later the jet engine, put an end to any possible viable use of this beautiful aircraft. It was scrapped in 1953.

THE BRISTOL BRABAZON ON TEST

In flight the Brabazon looked superb; on the ground she looked massive, and her first flight gave the impression that with proposed turbo-prop engines she would be an all-time winner. She was equipped with thirty seats to enable demonstration flights to be given, to show what travelling in a very large aircraft could be like. This resulted in interest being shown by BEA for a high-density aircraft for use on flights to the South of France, but sadly the whole project was abandoned when serious metal fatigue was discovered. Over half a century later, those of us who remember seeing her in flight are still intensely proud of her.

THE US AIR FORCE PEOPLE AND CARGO MOVERS

Douglas C74 Globemaster

The theme of only including civil airliners in this book has been varied to include the two American 'people movers' on this page. Both products of war, they were such extraordinary aircraft that the temptation to include them was too much to resist. The C47, above, was hated by the pilots and the engineers who maintained them, but when built they were the largest heavier-than-air aircraft flying and they certainly did the task required of them well enough. In 1949 one set up a record that can't be beaten: it became the first heavier-than-air machine to fly more than a hundred passengers across the North Atlantic. For its size, its maximum speed was a creditable 328 m.p.h. and at a cruise speed of 212 m.p.h. it had a range of over 7,000 miles which in those days was quite remarkable.

Douglas C133 Cargomaster

The turbo-prop Cargomaster entered service in 1956 and was built in small numbers as a logistic support aircraft. There are notes that on more than one occasion it carried well over 200 troops over Viet-Nam before being retired with fatigue problems.

SWORDS TO PLOUGHSHARES

In the mid and late 1940s British and American airlines made the best of the materials and experience available after the war to make a quick return to civil aviation with suitable pressurised aircraft. Boeings developed their Strato Fortress bomber into the Stratocruiser airliner (above) and BOAC acquired a number of them for their own routes. In the UK Avro, Bristol and Handley Page all used the same techniques to produce civilian aircraft and Handley Page's effort was the Hermes, seen in the picture below, which served BOAC well until it was superseded by later developments.

POST-WAR DOUGLAS AIRLINERS

In the ten years prior to the end of the Second World War, Douglas Aircraft had produced well over 12,000 aircraft including 10,000+ of the seemingly everlasting DC3, generally known as the Dakota. The DC4 was in effect a stretched, four-engined aircraft designed as an improvement on the DC3 and flown by dozens of airlines, including BOAC, as the 'Argonaut' and later converted for other British airlines as the 'Carvair'. Others were in turn stretched, pressurised and re-engined to become the DC6, shown below, and later still the DC7, all to serve the world over. A truly remarkable range of aircraft.

LOCKHEED CONSTELLATION

The Constellation was one of the world's great airliners, first designed by Howard Hughes in 1939 for use on his airline TWA. It first flew in 1943 but like many of Hughes' designs it was so far ahead of its time which, together with the inhibiting factor of World War II, delayed its real heyday until the 1950s. After the war it was hailed as the best and most beautiful four-engined propeller airliner by its passengers, aircrew and operators all over the world.

Over 850 were built in a dozen or more different configurations and it stayed popular as a passenger carrier until superseded by turbine and jet aircraft. TWA operated more 'Connies' than any other airline, some versions having a cruising speed of 300 m.p.h. It had a range in some configurations of five and a half thousand miles. It gave service into the 1960s when old age got the better of it, but it still remained to give service the world over in other capacities for a further two decades or more.

BRISTOL BRITANNIA – THE WHISPERING GIANT

After the fiasco of the Brabazon, the Bristol Aircraft Company produced a winning design in the 'Bristol Britannia'. Sad as it may seem, this superb aircraft never got its full market potential, mainly due to suffering from inept management of the late 1940s – not so much from Bristol, but through delivery of the needed power units being too little and too late.

It entered passenger service in the late 1950s and eventually, by the time the Proteus engines of sufficient power did become available, versions with a capacity of up to 99 passengers were built and transatlantic flights were possible. Airlines all over the world bought them; even the RAF bought and operated twenty-five Britannias in a variety of rôles, including many on VIP and Royal flights. Eventually technology overtook the Britannia, although it continued to serve in less glamorous rôles for three decades.

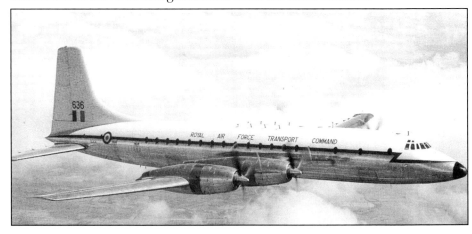

VICKERS VISCOUNT

It is probably true to say that the Vickers Viscount was the best of all the turbo-prop airliners ever built. Introduced in the mid-1950s, it made an instant impact on the commercial airliner market, even to the extent that the American dominance of it, if not completely shattered, was severely dented. Nearly five decades later there are still a couple of dozen of these highly successful aircraft operating, and even now they retain their popularity for comfortable, silky-smooth air transport.

Over four hundred and fifty Viscounts were built and were seen in service with airlines the world over. It was the neither the biggest nor the fastest 'people mover' in service when introduced – the latest variants had a maximum capacity for over eighty passengers and a cruising speed well over 400 m.p.h. – but is included here because it was an outstanding British civil aircraft of any age.

LOCKHEED L188 ELECTRA AND
VICKERS VANGUARD

Lockheed Electra

The Lockheed Electra and the Vickers Vanguard were both fine aircraft and had one thing in common – they were designed in the late 1950s to be the last word in passenger-carrying turbo-prop airliners. The Electra was meant to be 'one up' on the Viscount and Britannia but suffered a series of misfortunes and its entry into service was eclipsed by the development of jets, although many gave good service around the world. The Vanguard, in many ways similar to the Electra and a development of the Viscount, also suffered from being out-shone by jets. BEA and a Canadian airline operated forty or more of these aircraft, which continued to give service in freight capacities for several decades after their introduction. Both however were comfortable and popular 'people movers' for three or more decades.

Vickers Vanguard (later to be re-named 'Merchantman')

JETS RULE, OK

Nine De Havilland Comet jet airliners entered service in 1952 and were an immediate success with passengers and BOAC. Then disaster struck with unexplained losses which forced their withdrawal. After some years, tests revealed the cause and the Comets 2, 3 and 4 were built in some numbers, regaining their reputation for being very fine aircraft. While Comets were being redesigned other constructors, notably Boeing, began to churn out hundreds of newer, faster aircraft with a greater capacity that established the dominance of jet-powered aircraft in the medium and long haul routes.

The original doubts about the viability of jet aircraft were based on noise and fuel consumption. With hindsight it can now be seen that noise was certainly one strong and reasonable objection, especially from the public living under flight paths. Initially it seemed that noise could be overcome by installing so called 'hush kits', after which technological development took a hand.

Engines became larger, notably in diameter, which meant that blades of the turbines were greater and because the blade tips were not trying to go supersonic they were not only more efficient and powerful but quieter.

The increase in power has gone hand in hand with economy, power output and quietness to the extent that what we affectionately called 'Jumbo Jets' are now still 'jumbo' in terms of size, capacity, economy and range but only need two engines to do it. All these advantages have been incorporated into very small 'people movers' with carrying capacity of up to a hundred passengers on many routes where airfield size and passenger demands do not warrant larger aircraft.

Three decades ago a little bit of one-upmanship was to boast that your holiday was via a 'Jet to the Med'. This is no boast now as the chances are you will take a jet to nearly everywhere. Flying anywhere is not the exception these days, rather the accepted thing. This social change has made such a revolution in travel that with modern airports ninety per cent of travellers do not even see the outside of the aircraft; their first glimpse is of the cabin when they step on board straight from a departure lounge. Many have no idea of what type of aircraft they are in and only remember the in-flight movie, quality of the meal served or the leg room of their seat.

One thing is certain: in the normal course of events 'people moving' by air is here to stay, and it is many of the minor details that can stand improvement. Take a look at the Airbus A380 – it is probably aviation's 'people mover' for the next few decades.

THE DH COMET 4

The first Comet four-engined jet airliner flew in 1949 and great hopes were placed on this British achievement. Nine entered service in 1952 and proved popular until some unexplained fatal accidents forced their withdrawal. After a lengthy series of tests identified the problem as fatigue fractures around cabin windows, a new version, the Comet 2 (and later the 4) was introduced in 1958. This very successful aircraft inaugurated the first transatlantic jet flights with a Boeing 707 in October of that year – the Comet westwards and the 707 eastwards. The RAF had ten or more in service as the Comet 2 and a number of airlines operated the Comet 4 version on a variety of routes and charters before the type was superseded by more modern aircraft.

TUPOLEV TU104 ROSSIYA

The Tupolev was a remarkable aircraft by any standards and when introduced in the mid-1950s the aviation world had never seen anything like it before, and certainly had to sit up and take notice. It stemmed from the well-known Russian reconnaissance aircraft known in the Western World as the 'Bear'. It filled the need for a long distance major transport in Soviet Russia and was built on the direct instruction of Russia's then dictator Joseph Stalin for that purpose. It had four very powerful turbo-prop engines, each driving two contra-rotating propellers. Normally it carried 170 passengers although its maximum capacity was well over 200, with a flight crew of five and cabin crew of three stewardesses and two cooks! Its military origins showed in its civil performance speed of 475 miles per hour and range of 5,000+ miles.

THE VICKERS VC10

The prototype VC10 first flew in 1962 and two years later entered service with BOAC on their Nigerian route. This superb aircraft did everything asked of it and in many ways better. It was much loved and praised by operators, pilots and passengers alike, but in spite of this the market was flooded by American products with established world-wide support facilities and didn't sell to the market in sufficient quantities to make it a commercial success. In a number of versions it was popular wherever it flew and the RAF operated them for many years; even today they have a number serving as tankers, which says much for the high quality of the VC10 as an aircraft.

THE VC10 – THE JET WE LOVED

As many have said, a plane that looks good is good. While this is not always correct, the VC10 did come into that type of aircraft because when seen in the air it looked superb. The engines at the rear made the passengers happy because the cabin was less noisy, but more importantly it left the wings clear to do what wings do best, give the aircraft lift and controlability.

THE BOEING 707

The first Boeing 707 flew in 1954, eight years after World War II, and became a serious rival that soon overshadowed the British Comet. This is not surprising as it had nearly double the capacity and was faster. However, it has to be said that the USA had an internal demand for an aircraft of this nature that had no real equivalent in the rest of the Western World. The result was, and to a great extent still is, a home market for Boeings for hundreds and the rest of the world's customers in dozens. The economics of this situation are self explanatory and, to coin a phrase, 'Boeings rule, OK'. The 707 set the pattern and pace for the world.

THE BOEING 720

To the uninitiated the 707s and 720s were very similar, but it was the great flexibility of the 707 that made possible the variation to suit a different need: high density, medium and short haul routes. This was achieved by shortening the fuselage by nine feet, lightening the structure and making alterations to the wings. These savings enabled a greater passenger capacity and more economical operation over the shorter routes. An example of the somewhat denser passenger seating is shown below – a prelude to wide bodies?

THE BOEING 737

The Boeing 737 earns a place on these pages, not because of its size or performance, but because of the sheer numbers – well over two thousand – that have been built since 1967. Today, thirty-four years later, 1,500 are still flying with over a hundred airlines all over the world. As a medium-range airliner (some variants having a passenger capacity of 150 or more) it does rate high as aviation's 'people mover' of the present age.

There can be very few major or regional airports in the UK that have not seen the arrival and departure of a 737 and its dominance of the market for which it was built was not challenged for twenty years until the arrival of the Airbus A320, and the betting is that it will be at least another two decades before either of them is displaced.

HAWKER SIDDELEY TRIDENT

Originally a De Havilland aircraft, the Trident was introduced into BEA in 1964 to compete with the Caravelle. It was a fast, short-haul aircraft with a capacity of 160 to 180 passengers on many European and internal services. Because of the rather special requirements of BEA the Trident did not find favour with many overseas airlines, but orders were taken from a Chinese line and Cyprus. One of the unique claims made for the Trident was that on a BEA flight from Heathrow to Glasgow the first fully automatic landing was made with passengers on board.

BOEING 727

The Boeing 727, like many other Boeing airliners, deserves a book in its own rights. A 'people mover' it certainly was, and still is, serving with more airlines than we have room to mention on these pages. Between the first flight in 1963 and 1984, over 1,800 were built of this medium-range aircraft which, with a passenger capacity of just short of 200 in most of its variants, made it one of the greats.

The design was so flexible that not only were some built as freighters from the start, but other versions were configured for a 'quick change act' so that they had the capability of carrying passengers or cargo, using a large door and palletised passenger seats.

RUSSIA'S TRI JET – THE TUPOLEV TU154

While the 'Berlin Wall' syndrome was affecting East/West international relations, the Soviet Union was steadily building up fleets of very efficient aircraft to serve the needs of its vast hinterland. Like many developments of the era, Tupolev relied heavily on technology used in military designs but wasn't above using features used in western aircraft and owed some of these to the Boeing 727. The TU154 was a very successful aircraft on medium-haul routes demanding what was for the time a high capacity, and carried up to 168 passengers on many of their internal routes. This type of 'people mover' also found a market for the TU154 with their Eastern Bloc allies.

DOUGLAS DC8 AND McDONNELL DOUGLAS MD11

The Douglas Company stretched and stretched the DC8 until it couldn't be stretched any further and then produced a wide-bodied, long-range, three-engined jetliner (below) in conjunction with the McDonnell Company and adopted the designation 'MD' to replace the traditional DC (Douglas Commercial) designation. The result is the now named MD11.

These will be in service for many years to come as they will obviously replace the larger 'jumbo' jets over routes where the passenger density is not so great.

DOUGLAS DC10 AND LOCKHEED TRISTAR

It is easy to see the thinking that went on amongst major aircraft manufacturers when it became obvious that the faithful four-engined jets were not filling the need for high-density seating over the majority of medium distance routes. Wide body jets became 'the thing' and even these were soon the subject of intense development to adapt this revenue-earning feature to as many routes as possible. The 'Jet to the Med' syndrome became 'Jet to Everywhere'. The DC10 and Tristar were just the beginning.

THE BOEING 747

The Boeing 747, the first of the 'jumbo' jets, made its maiden flight in 1969, since when over a thousand have been built and flown all over the world. When introduced it astounded the world, and the media soon ran out of superlatives to describe it. The affectionate name 'jumbo jet' is still applied particularly to the 747 thirty years later. Even so, hardly a year goes by when the figures first recorded aren't still being modified as improved or special applications are called for to increase capacity and performance. The result is many dozens of variants and some present-day versions can carry over 500 passengers over many routes. Other versions can cover well over 300 passengers in comfort over 8,000 miles non-stop at an average in excess of 500 miles per hour. There is no room on these pages to give details of every version, so just two are shown – a long-range (SP) version (above), and the more common high capacity (747.400) below.

BOEING 747 AND FLIGHT DECK

The 747 Jumbo has been one of aviation's giant strides in 'people moving'. Technology has made possible larger versions, longer versions and shorter versions – all tailored to adapt to different customers' requirements. These variations have introduced significant differences in the aerodynamic handling of the various versions, which Boeing solved in a very practical way. This was to adjust the electronic control system (fly-by-wire), as seen in the picture below, to give pilots the same feel whichever version they are flying.

AIRBUS 340

Although the A340 Airbus has a smaller passenger capacity (about 340 to 375) than the Boeing 747.400 which can carry up to 550, it has been launched to cater for the very long distance routes that do not normally demand the greater capacity of the Boeing. With this slot in the market, with possible ranges of up to and in excess of 6,000 miles, the Airbus is presenting serious European competition to Boeing. First service flights began in the early 1990s and at the time of writing in 2001 orders and production had exceeded three hundred aircraft of the 330 and 340 variants, including aircraft for TWA who bought them to enable a non-stop service to fly from the US west coast to Europe.

HELICOPTERS AS PEOPLE MOVERS

Helicopters are not generally thought of as 'people movers' and I can only find one place where they are referred to as airliners. More frequently they are considered in a military function, but in fact the two types shown on this page move hundreds of people around the UK on a daily basis.

The Puma, shown above, and the S61 (below) move staff to and from oil and gas rigs around our coast. The inter-airport link between Heathrow and Gatwick is no longer operative, but a service is still maintained to the Scilly Islands from Penzance. The Puma above was operated by Bond Helicopters from Blackpool to the Morecambe Bay rigs and large numbers of many types fly on a regular basis from a number of East Coast airfields to the rigs in the North Sea. Naval, RAF and Bristow Helicopters also have a number on standby at points around the British Isles to operate search and rescue services offshore, and Mountain Rescue services.

AIRBUS 300 AND BOEING 767

Airbus 300

The fear of two-engined aircraft of earlier decades was well behind to the extent that wide-bodied two-engined aircraft with remarkable ranges and carrying capacity were regarded as normal in the 1990s and through to the present decade. The Airbus 300, above, can take up to 350 passengers well over 5,000 miles non-stop at a cruising speed of 555 miles per hour. It is in fact strong competition for the Boeing 767, seen below, which has a normal capacity for over 250 passengers with a remarkable range of up to 9,000 miles.

Boeing 767

AIRBUS 310 AND BOEING 757

Airbus 310

In the late 1980s and 1990s a new breed of aircraft started to emerge and dominate the skies. In a strange sort of way the attitude of those travelling by sea five decades earlier began to emerge again. In those days sea travellers regarded a ship with the most funnels as the best. In the 1980s and '90s many thought that travelling in aircraft with four engines was safer than those with only two. However, the fantastic development in power and economy of engines, together with modern airports, meant that few passengers ever saw the outside of aircraft until they saw it depart onwards once they had alighted. The Airbus 310 and Boeing 757 were two of this new breed. Both flew at over 550 miles per hour and both had non-stop ranges between 5,000 and 9,000 miles with loads of between 250 and 350 passengers.

Boeing 757

CONCORDE SUPERSONIC TRAVEL BY
BRITISH AIRWAYS AND AIR FRANCE

The first Concorde flight was by one of the Toulouse-built aircraft in 1969, followed a little later by a British-built one. Passenger services started in 1976 and continued until 2000, when an accident to a French-built machine on take-off led to all being grounded for modifications. At the time of writing tests were being carried out which look as if the type's certificate of airworthiness will be renewed and supersonic services restarted in the autumn of 2001.

CONCORDE IN HER ELEMENT

The Concorde shows off her sleek lines when flying supersonic above clouds, but one of the more amazing things about this aircraft is the sheer complexity of actually handling a sophisticated supersonic flying machine. Perhaps more amazing still is that the basic flying instruments such as the airspeed indicator, height indicator, rate of climb meter, artificial horizon and turn and bank indicator are all in the same basic six-instrument layout instantly recognised by the thousands of private pilots of today.

The Flight Deck

Tupolev produced some fifteen of the TU144, the first flight being made in December 1968. The first service flights were cargo only in 1975 and passenger flights were introduced in 1977. These were withdrawn after some problems a year later and abandoned. There has been recent activity when one or two of those which were not scrapped have been re-engined in co-operation with American interests, and other major modifications have been made.

THE WORLD'S LARGEST AIRCRAFT

The Antonov 225 Cossack was developed in 1988 from the slightly smaller An124 Condor and is the largest aircraft flying today. It was designed to transport Buran spacecraft on its back and is seen in the picture above on short final approach to Farnborough's air show, where it overshadowed everything else on the field. The picture below shows the ramp over which their cargoes of space shuttles are loaded.

AVIATION'S FUTURE IN PEOPLE MOVING?

On looking at the last century one has to come to two conclusions: one, that powered manned flight has developed from nothing into what we see today and two, regretfully, that had it not been for two World Wars aviation would not be what it is now.

However, true as those conclusions are, the 'up' side is that we also have the fusion of brain power around the globe, due to the tremendous advances in communications and digital technology that have given us modern computers. These machines have enabled aircraft manufacturers to design and produce aircraft to a specified performance with the almost certain knowledge that they will fly within the predicted limits.

The pages of this book have to a large extent been confined to a selection of the larger passenger aircraft, and a peep into the future was provided within the very year these pages were written. This was the announcement by Airbus Industries of the A3XX. The very day these words were being put to paper it was announced that the 3XX would be known as the A380 and that the company had orders for 50 aircraft of this design for delivery within five years – plus an indication of a further 21 options for delivery in the next five years.

Such is the confidence in the ability of aircraft manufacturers now that these orders were straight from the drawing board – or should that now be from the computer's memory? Further details of this boost to the European aviation industry are shown on some of the following pages.

Space flight is another prospect for the near future. It is already fact, but hardly in the field of mass 'people moving' and therefore we can only mention it in passing in this book. Another form of possible 'people moving' by air will probably cause a few raised eyebrows. This concerns the re-introduction for a variety of uses of airships. One will be forgiven for thinking the last of these fantastic aircraft had gone for ever after the Hindenburg disaster, but the facts are airships are being produced now and their size is increasing as well as the variety of uses to which they are being put. Technology has made them safe and, humans being what they are, they have put their brains to work to apply these great improvements in design to good use. There is at least one project for an airship with a capacity for a few hundred or more passengers, or a considerable load of cargo.

As we make no pretence at being prophets, the next few pages will serve to give a glimpse into the future as far as we can see it.

PROBABLY THE ULTIMATE IN AVIATION PEOPLE MOVERS FOR THE NEXT THIRTY YEARS

The Farnborough Air Show of 2000 saw a proposal for the introduction of Airbus A3XX. The proposal was for an aircraft that could carry up to 555 passengers non-stop for 8,500 miles. The problems of looking after that many passengers on a flight of this length gave rise to a number of radical ideas such as a duty free shop and lounge bars. There was immediate interest from Middle Eastern countries as well as firm orders with delivery promised for 2006, for this and a cargo version with a capacity for a load of 150 tonnes. Other features include a flight deck that has much in common with the Airbus A319.

THE AIRBUS 380

The Airbus has at the time of writing fifty orders on its books straight from the drawing board for the proposed A380. The picture above of how she will probably appear in Virgin colours can be considered as a glimpse into the not so distant future. If Virgin do what they plan it seems that something of the comfort and service which passengers used to receive in the days of Imperial Airways and flying boats will return to flying.

The flight deck shown below is actually that of an Airbus 340, but a few years ago it was also futuristic. The controls go back to the old idea of control stick, only today it controls the aircraft entirely through electronic systems, indeed fly-by-wire! Even the instruments are reduced to a few easily seen screens that give a comprehensive display of the aircraft's status from moment to moment.

Airbus Flight Deck

SPACE SHUTTLE – THE FASTEST OFF EARTH

The space shuttle may not be the largest aircraft to fly, but it is certainly the fastest once it leaves the atmosphere. The flight deck shown above is monitored by human aircrew, but the flying is normally done by computers. The launch is 'piggy back' on the rocket system and separation is made to place the orbiter in the exact orbit required for completion of the allotted mission. Once the crew has completed its tasks the computer again takes over and controls the re-entry into the atmosphere to complete what an aircraft pilot would call a 'dead stick' landing.

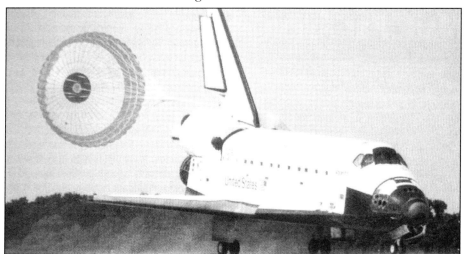

A FUTURE IN AIRSHIPS?

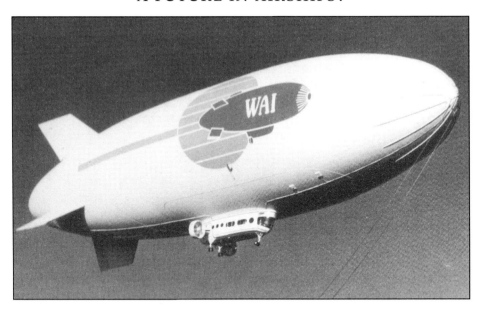

Above, a Westinghouse product in the Sentinal series, of which a number have been built and flown, mainly for military use. Below is one of British design which has become a popular sight over UK skies. Even larger ships are envisaged for some particular routes and the revival of airships has now become a strong possibility for particular applications. The public attitude to the disasters of the nineteen thirties is very understandable and were due to two factors which have now been overcome. These are the use of non inflammable helium gas and new and sophisticated control systems which make handling of these large aircraft a matter of routine.

ANOTHER GLIMPSE INTO THE FUTURE?

There were over thirty airships in service and flying regularly at the turn of the century, with another dozen or so on order. There is a project for a real giant to carry 160 tonnes of freight, expected to be flying in the year 2001. This will be a very large 'pie in the sky' indeed, but there are also a number with more modest capacity already on order and being built as fifty-two seaters.

The above is not all 'pie in the sky' because the five-seat AT10 seen here is not the largest type flying now.

It is not too much stretch of imagination to see how one of this sort of capacity could operate a 'park and ride shuttle' from, say, Kendal or Penrith to the very heart of the England's Lakeland. It would be quiet, safe and need little in the way of ground facilities. This is not the only tourist area where such a facility would be practical for 'people moving' as well as certain types of freight. Areas such as National Parks would welcome any moves to remove traffic from the roads, and in this country, say, travel to the Isle of Wight could present such a use for new types of airships.

It is fair to say there could be problems but over the centuries we seem to have managed to overcome most, which leaves this glimpse at possibilities looking more and more like a probable 'people mover' again.

NO END

There cannot be an end to this book; the story is incomplete and there hasn't been enough space or information available to make it comprehensive or definitive. A sample selection of civil aircraft which in most cases have been used to transport people has been used to depict the trend and developments that have taken place in the eight decades up to the start of the 21st century.

Many excellent aircraft have had to be left out and the selection has in the main concentrated on the larger ones, because these are the types that are remembered as they have been seen in many parts of the world. In recent years a large number of medium and short range aircraft carry more passengers in one day than some of the giants do in a week because, on the intensive shorter stages and to make them pay, they must be kept flying for as much of their life as is possible.

In many cases the aircraft used on these shorter stages are similar to those on the longer stages and use smaller regional airfields with less sophisticated navigational aids than those available at the international airports. This does not mean lesser safety standards because each of these airfields has very definite parameters under which they can and cannot be used.

These smaller airfields, or those that are not on or used by international routes, are well served by a multitude of aircraft types designed for such routes, some with such features as the ability to conform to short take-off and landing and noise abatement requirements. There are some aircraft depicted in this book which can and do serve the more regional airports, but because of the large numbers of these types, due purely to lack of space, we have had to be selective and omit many that perform the task of 'civil aviation's people movers' equally well.

There may be a case for another edition to cover a further selection featuring 'bus stop' type aircraft, for they are an equal and growing part of enabling a greater number of people to be moved from A to B by air.

In any case, while it is not possible to predict the future, the last hundred years has brought about civil aviation as we know it. So let us now look forward to what the future holds and, because it would seem that this book is only a look at the beginning, enjoy 'history in the making', for there is no end.

June 2001

ABOUT THE AUTHOR

Ken Davies was born in Cricklewood, London, in 1927 and educated at the Haberdashers Askes's School in Hampstead and later after the outbreak of World War II at the Torquay Grammar School.

In 1943, on leaving school, he joined the BBC as a Trainee Transmitter Engineer at a local transmitting station in Torquay. A year later he was posted to the Skelton transmitter in Cumbria, serving there until 1953 with a break for National Service between 1945 and 1948 when he became a Technical Sergeant Radar Mechanic in REME. In 1948 he rejoined the BBC at Skelton on demobilisation, later transferring to the Television Service in 1953.

Ken married in Penrith in 1950 and two of his three children were born there before he moved south to television transmitting stations in South Wales, Brighton, the Isle of Wight and South Devon.

In 1957 Ken left the BBC to take up a post as Marine Communications Engineer Supervisor for the Kuwait Oil Company. After three years in Kuwait he took a further post as Senior Transmitter and Communications Supervisor for the West Nigerian TV and broadcasting network, which he held until 1962.

At the end of the Nigerian contract, after the Nigerian Independence, Ken obtained a post with the Radio Corporation of America as a Project Engineer on the BMEWS (Early Warning Radar System) in New Jersey, Alaska and North Yorkshire. He later transferred to the Corporation's Broadcast and Communications Division in capacity as Installation Engineer on various projects in Nigeria, Italy, Netherlands and Pakistan.

After a short illness in 1970 he became self-employed as a consultant for Closed Circuit Television system applications with industrial and security applications.

In 1979 he retired from electronic work and built up a small publishing business, based on his own output of transport-related subjects, local interest and semi-technical frequency guides. Since then he has published or had published over forty of his own books until retiring in 1993 to continue writing books and articles on subjects of interest to him.

His hobbies and interests have included swimming, sailing, flying (he held a private pilot's licence in the nineteen-seventies), reading, and writing articles and books on a number of subjects.

WHY THIS BOOK?

The Author's Acknowledgements and Excuses

It all started when I was invited by 'you know who' to 'tidy up all those' – 'those' being boxes, folders and cuttings accumulated over the years because I was certain they would come in useful some time.

Reluctantly I set about the allotted task and was diverted, ever so slightly you will realise. The initial diversion was to put to one side pictures of all the aircraft types I had flown or flown in. It was then pointed out to me that my father started flying in 1916, and one of my grandchildren called us on his mobile while we were enjoying a pre-Christmas get-together in a 'local' last December. He told us he had just arrived in Cape Town to enjoy a week's good cricket before starting a new job in the New Year.

That call made me realise how much, in three generations of my immediate family, we had progressed since my father had started flying in the 'string and sealing wax' days. My own experience as a passenger started in the mid-1930s. I progressed to having flown all over the world in over forty different types of aircraft and with a few hundred hours as a private pilot. Now the whole family tend to think less about flying than they do about getting on a bus in these days of near universal car ownership.

This gave me the idea of sorting many of 'those' out – without being too biographical – into what I now claim is a brief outline of eight decades of 'people-moving by air'. It is not intended to be a history or technical treatise, but an illustrated sequence of development in civil airliners over their first eighty years of existence. The selection of illustrations has been collected over many years, never properly catalogued and without any intention originally of using them in anything likely to be published.

The result is that I really don't know their origins, and a few of them are not of what I could ever call first-class quality; they have been included because of the subject matter, illustrating the theme of the book. However, I have since seen quite a few in other publications, many with different credits in different publications. Equally, I know that a few have never before been published and I sincerely hope that those donors who responded to my requests for 'pictures to add to my collection' will be pleased to see them included on some of these pages.

I have deliberately omitted military aircraft unless there has been a strong case of them being used as transport for people, as others have covered that aspect of flying much better than I could ever hope to. It has certainly given me a lot of pleasure and at the same time taught me much of when, what and why 'people-moving by air' has developed in the way it has. If others browsing through these pages find as much interest, memories and enjoyment as I have in collating them, I will be well satisfied.

Ken Davies, 2001

BY THE SAME AUTHOR

1978	UK Radio Station Guide Cards
1980	UK Radio Station Guide Cards *(2nd edition)*
1980	The Clyde Passenger Steamer
1980/2/4	UK Airband Guide *(3 editions)*
1983	Solent Passages and Their Steamers
1983	Companion to the Fylde
1983	Motorists' Guide to Good Listening
1984/5	Radio On The Move *(2 editions)*
1984	Air Traffic Radio in NW England
1984	English Lakeland Steamers
1985/6/91/2/5	Air Traffic Radio *(5 editions)*
1985	Cumbria's Fringe Benefits
1985	Windmill Trails of the Fylde
1987	Wessex Coast Ferries and Pleasure Craft
1987	Radio On The Move *(5th edition)*
1987	UK Coastal Radio Services
1989	Safety Call Charts *(12 charts)*
1991/2	Sounds Easy *(1st edition)*
1992	New Forest Airfields
1992	90 Days to Normandy
1992	Solent Ferries and Vectis Connections
1992	Sandown, An Island's Airport
1993/5	Air to Ground *(2 editions)*
1992	Skelton Transmitting Station Facsimile
1994	Waterbuses to Warships
1994	The Lost Seaport of Titchfield and its Canal
1995	Cumbrian-built Ships
1995	Skelton, Penrith and The World *(2 editions)*
1998	Frigates and Ferries
1998	The Titchfield Canal
2000	A Century of Lakeland Aviation
2000	Lakeland Pleasure Craft
2000	Lakeland's Fringes
2000	Solent Shipping Viewpoints
2000	Solent Nostalgia
2000	Windmill Land of Lancashire
2000	Titchfield's Canal *(2nd edition)*
2001	Lakeland Pleasure Craft
2001	Lakeland Aviation and Airfields in the 20th Century